# 50 Caramel Dishes for Home

By: Kelly Johnson

# Table of Contents

- Caramel Popcorn
- Caramel Apples
- Salted Caramel Brownies
- Caramel Pudding
- Caramel Cheesecake
- Caramel Flan
- Caramel Sauce
- Caramel Ice Cream
- Caramel Cupcakes
- Caramel Latte
- Caramelized Bananas
- Caramel Shortbread Bars
- Caramel Apple Pie
- Caramel Sticky Buns
- Caramel Churros
- Caramel Macchiato
- Caramel Fudge
- Caramelized Nuts
- Caramel Bread Pudding
- Caramel Pretzel Bark
- Caramel Cornflake Bars
- Caramel Blondies
- Caramel Éclairs
- Caramel Mousse
- Caramel Tiramisu
- Caramel Layer Cake
- Caramel Crème Brûlée
- Caramel Rice Krispie Treats
- Caramel Pecan Pie
- Caramel Donuts
- Caramel Chocolate Tart
- Caramelized Pears
- Caramelized Onions
- Caramel Peanut Butter Cups
- Caramel Truffles

- Caramel Yogurt Parfait
- Caramel Sticky Rice
- Caramelized Pineapple
- Caramelized Fig Tart
- Caramel Nut Clusters
- Caramel Apple Crisp
- Caramel Buttercream Frosting
- Caramelized Brussels Sprouts
- Caramel Pancakes
- Caramelized Sweet Potatoes
- Caramelized Bacon
- Caramel Chocolate Chip Cookies
- Caramel Glazed Chicken
- Caramelized Peaches
- Caramel Mocha

## Caramel Popcorn

**Ingredients:**

- 10 cups popped popcorn
- 1 cup sugar
- ½ cup butter
- ½ cup corn syrup
- ½ tsp salt
- ½ tsp baking soda
- 1 tsp vanilla

**Instructions:**

1. Preheat oven to 250°F (120°C). Place popcorn in a large bowl.
2. In a saucepan, heat sugar, butter, corn syrup, and salt over medium heat. Boil for 5 minutes, stirring occasionally.
3. Remove from heat, add baking soda and vanilla, and stir.
4. Pour caramel over popcorn, mix, then spread on a lined baking sheet.
5. Bake for 45 minutes, stirring every 15 minutes.

**Caramel Apples**

**Ingredients:**

- 6 apples
- 1 cup sugar
- ½ cup butter
- ½ cup heavy cream
- ½ cup corn syrup
- 1 tsp vanilla
- Pinch of salt

**Instructions:**

1. Wash and dry apples, then insert wooden sticks.
2. Heat sugar, butter, cream, corn syrup, and salt over medium heat, stirring until caramel thickens.
3. Remove from heat, stir in vanilla, and let cool slightly.
4. Dip apples in caramel, place on parchment paper, and let set.

**Salted Caramel Brownies**

**Ingredients:**

- 1 cup butter, melted
- 1 cup sugar
- ½ cup cocoa powder
- 2 eggs
- 1 tsp vanilla
- ¾ cup flour
- ½ tsp salt
- ½ cup caramel sauce
- ½ tsp sea salt

**Instructions:**

1. Preheat oven to 350°F (175°C). Grease a baking pan.
2. Mix butter, sugar, cocoa, eggs, and vanilla.
3. Stir in flour and salt, then pour batter into the pan.
4. Drizzle caramel over batter and swirl with a knife.
5. Sprinkle sea salt on top and bake for 25 minutes.

## Caramel Pudding

**Ingredients:**

- ½ cup sugar
- 2 cups milk
- ¼ cup cornstarch
- ¼ tsp salt
- ½ cup caramel sauce
- 1 tsp vanilla

**Instructions:**

1. Heat sugar in a pan until melted and golden brown.
2. Gradually add milk, whisking until smooth.
3. Stir in cornstarch and salt, and cook until thickened.
4. Remove from heat, mix in caramel sauce and vanilla.
5. Chill before serving.

**Caramel Cheesecake**

**Ingredients:**

- 1 ½ cups graham cracker crumbs
- ¼ cup melted butter
- 16 oz cream cheese, softened
- ½ cup sugar
- 2 eggs
- 1 tsp vanilla
- ½ cup caramel sauce

**Instructions:**

1. Preheat oven to 325°F (160°C).
2. Mix crumbs and butter, press into a springform pan.
3. Beat cream cheese, sugar, eggs, and vanilla until smooth.
4. Pour over crust and bake for 45 minutes.
5. Cool, then drizzle with caramel sauce before serving.

**Caramel Flan**

**Ingredients:**

- ¾ cup sugar
- 2 cups milk
- 3 eggs
- 1 tsp vanilla

**Instructions:**

1. Melt sugar in a pan until golden caramel forms. Pour into ramekins.
2. In a bowl, whisk milk, eggs, and vanilla. Pour over caramel.
3. Bake in a water bath at 325°F (160°C) for 45 minutes.
4. Chill before inverting onto plates.

**Caramel Sauce**

**Ingredients:**

- 1 cup sugar
- ½ cup butter
- ½ cup heavy cream
- 1 tsp vanilla
- Pinch of salt

**Instructions:**

1. Heat sugar over medium heat until melted.
2. Stir in butter until combined.
3. Slowly add cream while stirring.
4. Remove from heat, mix in vanilla and salt.

**Caramel Ice Cream**

**Ingredients:**

- 1 cup sugar
- 2 cups heavy cream
- 1 cup milk
- 4 egg yolks
- 1 tsp vanilla

**Instructions:**

1. Melt sugar in a pan until golden.
2. Slowly whisk in cream and milk.
3. Beat egg yolks, then slowly add hot mixture while stirring.
4. Cook until thickened, then chill and churn in an ice cream maker.

**Caramel Cupcakes**

**Ingredients:**

- 1 ½ cups flour
- 1 cup sugar
- ½ cup butter
- 2 eggs
- 1 tsp vanilla
- ½ cup milk
- ½ cup caramel sauce

**Instructions:**

1. Preheat oven to 350°F (175°C).
2. Beat butter and sugar, then mix in eggs and vanilla.
3. Add flour and milk, mixing until smooth.
4. Divide into cupcake liners and bake for 18 minutes.
5. Drizzle with caramel sauce.

**Caramel Latte**

**Ingredients:**

- 1 cup milk
- 1 shot espresso (or ½ cup strong coffee)
- 2 tbsp caramel sauce
- Whipped cream (optional)

**Instructions:**

1. Heat milk until hot but not boiling. Froth if desired.
2. Brew espresso and mix with caramel sauce.
3. Pour hot milk over espresso and stir.
4. Top with whipped cream and extra caramel drizzle.

## Caramelized Bananas

**Ingredients:**

- 2 ripe bananas, sliced
- 2 tbsp butter
- ¼ cup brown sugar
- ½ tsp cinnamon

**Instructions:**

1. Melt butter in a pan over medium heat.
2. Add brown sugar and stir until dissolved.
3. Add banana slices and cook until caramelized, about 2 minutes per side.
4. Sprinkle with cinnamon and serve warm.

**Caramel Shortbread Bars**

**Ingredients:**

- 1 cup flour
- ½ cup butter, softened
- ¼ cup sugar
- ½ cup caramel sauce
- ½ cup chocolate chips (optional)

**Instructions:**

1. Preheat oven to 350°F (175°C).
2. Mix flour, butter, and sugar to form dough.
3. Press into a baking pan and bake for 15 minutes.
4. Spread caramel over the crust, then drizzle with melted chocolate.
5. Cool before slicing.

**Caramel Apple Pie**

**Ingredients:**

- 1 pie crust
- 5 apples, sliced
- ½ cup sugar
- 1 tsp cinnamon
- ¼ cup caramel sauce

**Instructions:**

1. Preheat oven to 375°F (190°C).
2. Toss apples with sugar and cinnamon.
3. Place in pie crust, drizzle caramel sauce over apples.
4. Cover with top crust, seal edges, and bake for 45 minutes.

**Caramel Sticky Buns**

**Ingredients:**

- 2 cups flour
- 1 tbsp yeast
- ½ cup milk
- ¼ cup sugar
- ¼ cup butter
- ½ cup caramel sauce
- ½ cup chopped nuts

**Instructions:**

1. Mix flour, yeast, milk, sugar, and butter to form dough. Let rise.
2. Roll out dough, spread caramel sauce and sprinkle nuts.
3. Roll up, slice into buns, and place in a greased pan.
4. Bake at 350°F (175°C) for 25 minutes.

**Caramel Churros**

**Ingredients:**

- 1 cup water
- ½ cup butter
- 1 tbsp sugar
- 1 cup flour
- 2 eggs
- ½ cup caramel sauce

**Instructions:**

1. Heat water, butter, and sugar until boiling.
2. Stir in flour and cook for 1 minute.
3. Remove from heat, beat in eggs.
4. Pipe dough into hot oil and fry until golden.
5. Drizzle with caramel sauce.

**Caramel Macchiato**

**Ingredients:**

- 1 cup milk
- 1 shot espresso
- 2 tbsp caramel sauce

**Instructions:**

1. Froth hot milk and pour into a cup.
2. Add caramel sauce and mix.
3. Pour espresso over the milk.

## Caramel Fudge

**Ingredients:**

- 2 cups sugar
- ½ cup butter
- ½ cup heavy cream
- 1 tsp vanilla

**Instructions:**

1. Heat sugar, butter, and cream until melted.
2. Boil for 5 minutes, then remove from heat and stir in vanilla.
3. Pour into a lined pan and let cool before cutting.

## Caramelized Nuts

**Ingredients:**

- 1 cup mixed nuts
- ½ cup sugar
- 1 tbsp butter
- ½ tsp salt

**Instructions:**

1. Melt sugar in a pan until golden.
2. Stir in nuts and butter.
3. Spread onto parchment paper to cool.

**Caramel Bread Pudding**

**Ingredients:**

- 4 cups bread cubes
- 2 cups milk
- ½ cup sugar
- 2 eggs
- ½ cup caramel sauce

**Instructions:**

1. Preheat oven to 350°F (175°C).
2. Mix milk, sugar, and eggs, then pour over bread cubes.
3. Let soak for 10 minutes, then drizzle with caramel sauce.
4. Bake for 35 minutes.

**Caramel Pretzel Bark**

**Ingredients:**

- 2 cups pretzels
- 1 cup caramel sauce
- 1 cup chocolate chips

**Instructions:**

1. Line a baking sheet with parchment paper.
2. Spread pretzels evenly on the sheet.
3. Drizzle caramel sauce over the pretzels.
4. Melt chocolate chips and drizzle over the caramel.
5. Let cool until set, then break into pieces.

## Caramel Cornflake Bars

**Ingredients:**

- 4 cups cornflakes
- ½ cup caramel sauce
- ¼ cup melted butter

**Instructions:**

1. Mix cornflakes with caramel sauce and melted butter.
2. Press into a greased baking dish.
3. Let set before cutting into bars.

**Caramel Blondies**

**Ingredients:**

- 1 cup butter, melted
- 1 cup brown sugar
- 2 eggs
- 1 tsp vanilla
- 1 ½ cups flour
- ½ cup caramel sauce

**Instructions:**

1. Preheat oven to 350°F (175°C).
2. Mix butter, sugar, eggs, and vanilla.
3. Stir in flour, then pour into a greased baking pan.
4. Swirl caramel sauce into the batter.
5. Bake for 25 minutes.

## Caramel Éclairs

**Ingredients:**

- 1 cup water
- ½ cup butter
- 1 cup flour
- 4 eggs
- 1 cup caramel pastry cream
- 1 cup caramel glaze

**Instructions:**

1. Preheat oven to 375°F (190°C).
2. Heat water and butter until melted, then stir in flour.
3. Remove from heat and beat in eggs one at a time.
4. Pipe onto a baking sheet and bake for 25 minutes.
5. Fill with caramel pastry cream and top with caramel glaze.

**Caramel Mousse**

**Ingredients:**

- 1 cup caramel sauce
- 1 cup heavy cream
- ½ tsp vanilla

**Instructions:**

1. Whip heavy cream until stiff peaks form.
2. Fold in caramel sauce and vanilla.
3. Chill before serving.

## Caramel Tiramisu

**Ingredients:**

- 1 cup caramel sauce
- 1 cup mascarpone cheese
- 1 cup whipped cream
- 1 cup coffee
- 12 ladyfingers

**Instructions:**

1. Mix mascarpone with caramel sauce and whipped cream.
2. Dip ladyfingers in coffee and layer with caramel mixture.
3. Repeat layers and chill before serving.

**Caramel Layer Cake**

**Ingredients:**

- 2 cups flour
- 1 cup sugar
- 1 cup butter
- 3 eggs
- ½ cup caramel sauce

**Instructions:**

1. Preheat oven to 350°F (175°C).
2. Mix flour, sugar, butter, and eggs.
3. Bake in greased cake pans for 30 minutes.
4. Spread caramel sauce between layers and over the cake.

**Caramel Crème Brûlée**

**Ingredients:**

- 2 cups heavy cream
- ½ cup caramel sauce
- 4 egg yolks

**Instructions:**

1. Preheat oven to 325°F (160°C).
2. Heat cream and caramel sauce until warm.
3. Whisk egg yolks and slowly mix in warm cream.
4. Pour into ramekins and bake in a water bath for 40 minutes.
5. Chill and caramelize sugar on top before serving.

**Caramel Rice Krispie Treats**

**Ingredients:**

- 4 cups Rice Krispies
- ½ cup caramel sauce
- ¼ cup butter
- 4 cups marshmallows

**Instructions:**

1. Melt butter and marshmallows over low heat.
2. Stir in caramel sauce and Rice Krispies.
3. Press into a greased pan and let cool before cutting.

**Caramel Pecan Pie**

**Ingredients:**

- 1 pie crust
- 1 cup pecans
- ½ cup caramel sauce
- 2 eggs
- ½ cup brown sugar

**Instructions:**

1. Preheat oven to 350°F (175°C).
2. Mix eggs, sugar, and caramel sauce.
3. Pour over pecans in the pie crust.
4. Bake for 40 minutes.

**Caramel Donuts**

**Ingredients:**

- 2 ½ cups flour
- ½ cup sugar
- 1 packet yeast
- ½ cup warm milk
- 1 egg
- ¼ cup melted butter
- 1 tsp vanilla
- 1 cup caramel sauce

**Instructions:**

1. Mix yeast with warm milk and let sit for 5 minutes.
2. Add flour, sugar, egg, butter, and vanilla, and knead into a dough.
3. Let rise for 1 hour, then roll and cut into donut shapes.
4. Fry until golden brown, then dip in caramel sauce.

## Caramel Chocolate Tart

**Ingredients:**

- 1 tart crust
- 1 cup caramel sauce
- 1 cup dark chocolate
- ½ cup heavy cream

**Instructions:**

1. Bake tart crust at 350°F (175°C) for 10 minutes.
2. Pour caramel sauce into the crust.
3. Melt chocolate with heavy cream and pour over caramel.
4. Chill before serving.

**Caramelized Pears**

**Ingredients:**

- 2 pears, sliced
- ¼ cup brown sugar
- 2 tbsp butter

**Instructions:**

1. Melt butter in a pan and add brown sugar.
2. Add pears and cook until golden and caramelized.

**Caramelized Onions**

**Ingredients:**

- 2 large onions, sliced
- 2 tbsp butter
- 1 tbsp sugar

**Instructions:**

1. Melt butter in a pan over low heat.
2. Add onions and sugar, and cook slowly until soft and caramelized.

**Caramel Peanut Butter Cups**

**Ingredients:**

- 1 cup chocolate, melted
- ½ cup peanut butter
- ¼ cup caramel sauce

**Instructions:**

1. Fill cupcake liners with a layer of melted chocolate.
2. Add a layer of peanut butter and caramel sauce.
3. Cover with more melted chocolate and chill.

**Caramel Truffles**

**Ingredients:**

- 1 cup caramel sauce
- 2 cups dark chocolate, melted
- ½ cup cocoa powder

**Instructions:**

1. Mix caramel sauce with melted chocolate.
2. Let chill, then roll into small balls.
3. Coat in cocoa powder.

**Caramel Yogurt Parfait**

**Ingredients:**

- 1 cup yogurt
- ½ cup granola
- ¼ cup caramel sauce

**Instructions:**

1. Layer yogurt, granola, and caramel sauce in a glass.

**Caramel Sticky Rice**

**Ingredients:**

- 1 cup sticky rice, cooked
- ½ cup coconut milk
- ¼ cup caramel sauce

**Instructions:**

1. Mix cooked rice with coconut milk and caramel sauce.

**Caramelized Pineapple**

**Ingredients:**

- 1 pineapple, sliced
- ¼ cup brown sugar
- 2 tbsp butter

**Instructions:**

1. Melt butter in a pan and add brown sugar.
2. Add pineapple slices and cook until caramelized.

**Caramelized Fig Tart**

**Ingredients:**

- 1 tart crust
- 1 cup caramel sauce
- 6 fresh figs, sliced

**Instructions:**

1. Bake tart crust at 350°F (175°C) for 10 minutes.
2. Pour caramel sauce into the crust and top with figs.
3. Bake for 10 more minutes.

**Caramel Nut Clusters**

**Ingredients:**

- 1 cup caramel sauce
- 1 ½ cups mixed nuts (almonds, pecans, cashews)
- 1 cup dark chocolate, melted

**Instructions:**

1. Line a baking sheet with parchment paper.
2. Drop small clusters of mixed nuts onto the sheet.
3. Drizzle caramel sauce over each cluster.
4. Pour melted chocolate over the top.
5. Let set until firm before serving.

## Caramel Apple Crisp

### Ingredients:

- 4 apples, sliced
- ½ cup caramel sauce
- ½ cup oats
- ½ cup brown sugar
- ¼ cup flour
- ½ tsp cinnamon
- ¼ cup butter, melted

### Instructions:

1. Preheat oven to 350°F (175°C).
2. Place apple slices in a baking dish and drizzle with caramel sauce.
3. In a bowl, mix oats, brown sugar, flour, cinnamon, and melted butter.
4. Sprinkle oat mixture over apples.
5. Bake for 30-35 minutes until golden brown.

**Caramel Buttercream Frosting**

**Ingredients:**

- 1 cup butter, softened
- 3 cups powdered sugar
- ½ cup caramel sauce
- 1 tsp vanilla extract
- 2 tbsp heavy cream

**Instructions:**

1. Beat butter until light and fluffy.
2. Add powdered sugar and mix until combined.
3. Pour in caramel sauce and vanilla extract.
4. Add heavy cream and whip until smooth.

**Caramelized Brussels Sprouts**

**Ingredients:**

- 1 lb Brussels sprouts, halved
- 2 tbsp butter
- 2 tbsp brown sugar
- 1 tbsp balsamic vinegar
- Salt and pepper to taste

**Instructions:**

1. Heat butter in a pan over medium heat.
2. Add Brussels sprouts and cook until golden brown.
3. Stir in brown sugar and balsamic vinegar.
4. Cook for 2-3 minutes until caramelized.

## Caramel Pancakes

### Ingredients:

- 1 ½ cups flour
- 1 tbsp sugar
- 1 tsp baking powder
- 1 tsp baking soda
- 1 ¼ cups buttermilk
- 1 egg
- 2 tbsp melted butter
- ½ cup caramel sauce

### Instructions:

1. Mix dry ingredients in a bowl.
2. Whisk in buttermilk, egg, and melted butter.
3. Cook pancakes on a hot griddle.
4. Drizzle with caramel sauce before serving.

## Caramelized Sweet Potatoes

### Ingredients:

- 3 sweet potatoes, cubed
- 3 tbsp butter
- ¼ cup brown sugar
- 1 tsp cinnamon
- 1 tbsp maple syrup

### Instructions:

1. Preheat oven to 375°F (190°C).
2. Toss sweet potatoes with melted butter, brown sugar, and cinnamon.
3. Spread on a baking sheet and roast for 30 minutes.
4. Drizzle with maple syrup before serving.

**Caramelized Bacon**

**Ingredients:**

- 8 slices bacon
- ¼ cup brown sugar
- 1 tbsp maple syrup
- ½ tsp black pepper

**Instructions:**

1. Preheat oven to 375°F (190°C).
2. Coat bacon with brown sugar and maple syrup.
3. Place on a baking rack and bake for 15-20 minutes until crispy.

## Caramel Chocolate Chip Cookies

**Ingredients:**

- 1 cup butter, softened
- 1 cup brown sugar
- ½ cup white sugar
- 2 eggs
- 2 tsp vanilla extract
- 2 ¼ cups flour
- 1 tsp baking soda
- 1 cup chocolate chips
- ½ cup caramel bits

**Instructions:**

1. Preheat oven to 350°F (175°C).
2. Beat butter and sugars until creamy.
3. Mix in eggs and vanilla.
4. Stir in flour and baking soda.
5. Fold in chocolate chips and caramel bits.
6. Scoop onto a baking sheet and bake for 10-12 minutes.

**Caramel Glazed Chicken**

**Ingredients:**

- 2 chicken breasts
- ¼ cup caramel sauce
- 1 tbsp soy sauce
- 1 tsp garlic powder
- ½ tsp black pepper

**Instructions:**

1. Preheat oven to 375°F (190°C).
2. Mix caramel sauce, soy sauce, garlic powder, and black pepper.
3. Coat chicken with the glaze and bake for 25-30 minutes.

**Caramelized Peaches**

**Ingredients:**

- 2 peaches, halved
- 2 tbsp butter
- 2 tbsp brown sugar
- ½ tsp cinnamon

**Instructions:**

1. Heat butter in a pan over medium heat.
2. Add peaches and sprinkle with brown sugar and cinnamon.
3. Cook until golden and caramelized.

**Caramel Mocha**

**Ingredients:**

- 1 cup hot coffee
- ½ cup milk
- 2 tbsp caramel sauce
- 2 tbsp cocoa powder
- Whipped cream (optional)

**Instructions:**

1. Heat milk and whisk in caramel sauce and cocoa powder.
2. Pour into hot coffee and stir well.
3. Top with whipped cream and extra caramel drizzle.

www.ingramcontent.com/pod-product-compliance
Lightning Source LLC
LaVergne TN
LVHW081332060526
838201LV00055B/2606